THE EUCHARISTIC LITURGY
OF TAIZÉ

THE EUCHARISTIC LITURGY OF TAIZÉ

WITH AN INTRODUCTORY ESSAY

BY MAX THURIAN
FRÈRE DE TAIZÉ

TRANSLATED BY JOHN ARNOLD

Distributed in the United States by

CHRISTIAN CLASSICS
205 Willis Street, Westminster, Md. 21157

FIRST PUBLISHED IN 1962
REPRINTED IN 1963
Translated from the French
EUCHARISTIE A TAIZÉ
© *1959 Les Presses de Taizé*
This translation © *The Taizé Community 1962*

PRINTED IN GREAT BRITAIN
in 11 point Garamond type
BY THE FAITH PRESS LTD.
LEIGHTON BUZZARD

CONTENTS

INTRODUCTORY ESSAY

THE CELEBRATION OF THE EUCHARIST

INTRODUCTION

The liturgical revival of the last few decades has led the Reformed Churches to rediscover the ancient structures and, sometimes too, the texts of the Western eucharistic-celebration. But although the structures and the texts have been restored, providing the Church with a number of very beautiful liturgies, the problem of celebration itself remains. As a result of a certain fear of forms and gestures, a liturgy which should be *experienced* is often only *said* or *sung*.

Here we should like to give some information about the Sunday celebration of the Holy Communion in the Taizé community. These notes are not purely documentary; they should help ministers and congregations to discover a more corporate form of celebration of their Sunday liturgy. Not that the Taizé community wishes to have its liturgy copied. What is suitable for the cenobitic life is probably not suitable for parish life. Moreover, due regard for church discipline precludes the making of innovations in the text and form of worship, which might offend and upset unprepared parishioners.

All we are trying to do here is to stimulate ministers and congregations to celebrate, perhaps more fully, the authorized liturgy of their church. We will describe quite simply the celebration of a community which is seeking, by means of the best possible participation in liturgical worship, to renew its life in the world. Again, it is not our intention in these notes to propose a new text. That would be to run the risk of creating anarchy. It is only a question of understanding a particular form of celebration, not in order to copy it, but in order to stimulate thought about ways of experiencing the Church's liturgy. One way of celebrating could be adopted in the parish; another might stimulate thought and lead to a happy adaptation; while yet another would be regarded as suitable only for a cenobitic community, and impossible in a parish.

At Taizé instruction has been given to the congregation on Sunday mornings before the liturgy for some time now; and we know from experience that many aspects of liturgical life, which might have seemed strange to some, became clear and simple. It is difficult to write about the liturgical life, because liturgy is something which should be experienced. This is an excuse for those who do not understand these lines, which are only intended to witness to the joy which God gives to him who, despite his wretchedness, seeks to 'look upon him in the sanctuary . . . with glad shouts and songs of thanksgiving, a multitude keeping festival' (Pss. 63 : 2; 42 : 4).

Royal Priesthood

Liturgy is the work of the whole people of God, in praise and prayer. Christ, our High Priest and heavenly Intercessor, has made us 'a kingdom, priests to his God and Father' (Rev. 1 : 6). The Father's family, taken as a whole, is 'a holy priesthood, to offer spiritual sacrifices acceptable to God through Jesus Christ' (1 Peter 2 : 5). Moreover, it is a characteristic of Christian worship that all should participate effectively in the liturgy.

The Taizé community is trying to recover the real participation of the whole community and the whole congregation in the liturgy, by organizing the officiants in such a way that each has his own task, which he performs in communion with the others. It is not a matter of having one ordained celebrant who alone is able to celebrate the liturgy, while the rest join in to some extent with canticles or responses. It is a matter of corporate celebration.

The celebrant is there for the sacrament, that is essentially to say the great eucharistic prayer. There are other elements of the liturgy which fall to him; but his primary task is to present the memorial of Christ, and to invoke the Holy Spirit in order

2

that God may actualize the mystery of redemption and give Himself to the Church in the Body and Blood of His Son.

The deacon in the Taizé liturgy is usually a lay brother. His function is to lead every one in prayer. The three proper prayers of the liturgy fall to him: the collect of the day after the Gloria, in preparation for the lections; the offertory prayer before the great eucharistic prayer; and the thanksgiving after communion. This is a novelty of the celebration at Taizé. In the traditional liturgy these prayers are reserved for the celebrant. The Taizé liturgy is in a particular tradition of the universal Church, the Western tradition; but it takes certain liberties, which seem to be important, if we are to increase the participation of many in the eucharistic celebration. This may be questioned, but it represents an approach to the answering of a need. As in all liturgical traditions, it is the deacon who reads the gospel. We shall see later that other elements of the celebration are also his.

The sub-deacon is responsible for the reading of the epistle, and for certain other elements of the celebration.

The lector reads the Old Testament lesson. Several cantors assist by intoning the antiphons and leading the singing. They are also the soloists in the singing of the propers of the liturgy.

Then there is the community, which really functions as a whole, and which enters into the celebration by singing the ordinaries: the Kyries, the Gloria, the Sanctus, the Agnus Dei; and some of the propers—the antiphons, the introit, the gradual after the Old Testament, the alleluia after the epistle, the offertory before the eucharistic prayer, and the communion during the distribution of the elements to the brothers and to the congregation. The community is also, on occasion, divided into two groups, in order to sing certain parts of the liturgy, especially the psalms, alternately or antiphonally.

These then are the officiants of the liturgy. They multiply and diversify the Church's liturgical ministry. This is a liturgical community, a celebrating community which functions at different moments in the liturgy through the celebrant, the deacon, the sub-deacon, the lector, etc.; it expresses the congregation, which in turn expresses the whole Church.

3

The celebrant is not an intermediary between the community or the Church and God. In the liturgy the whole community, the whole Church has access to the Father by virtue of the royal priesthood of all the baptized. Thus the whole community, arranged in its various ministries, has the right and the duty of offering its worship to God. This universal priesthood of the baptized in the liturgy is the fundamental reason for the active participation of all in the whole celebration. Moreover, since it is impossible for all the faithful to express their worship simultaneously throughout the service, this is sometimes done by one of the officiants. Thus the deacon expresses the intentions of all in the litany, the intercessions and the other prayers. The celebrant expresses the thanksgiving and the self-offering of all in the great eucharistic prayer. . . . But in all this the officiants are not intermediaries, approaching God in the place of others. That conception of worship belongs to the Old Covenant. By His sacrifice on the Cross, His death, His resurrection and His ascension, Christ became the one and only High Priest of the New Covenant. He offered the perfect sacrifice, the tokens of which He presents eternally in intercession in the heavenly sanctuary. Thus He is the only Mediator, by whom all the baptized have free access to the Father. The congregation demonstrates the universality of the royal priesthood of the baptized, by their active participation in the liturgy, of which Christ alone is the High Priest and Mediator before the Father. The officiants therefore do not have a mediatorial role between the Church and God, since Christ is the only High Priest and Mediator; all they do is to express prayer and praise which the church community cannot always express together. At certain moments during the liturgy they lend their voices and their gestures to the whole community, which expresses itself through them. They are simply members of the Church, commissioned by her to express her prayer and praise.

However, the liturgy is not only the expression of the intercession and thanksgiving of the Church. It is also an act of God, speaking to His people and revealing His presence. It is not only a movement from below upwards, but also, and primarily, a movement from above downwards. When the officiants read the

Word of God, preach, and perform sacramental acts they are no longer acting as the expression of the Church's prayer but as signs of Christ proclaiming the Word of God, and as signs of Christ manifesting His presence. If, in the first case, they are the expression of the Church's prayer, in the second they are instruments of Christ. In the first case they act as members of the Church, expressing the Church; in the second they act as ministers of Christ in and for His Church. In giving expression to the Church the officiants do not in any way take up a mediatorial position between the company of faithful people and its God; but, as instruments and signs of Christ, they do participate in His mediation between God and the Church. Without their ministry, the Word of God would not be truly proclaimed and preached, nor the sacrament of the Body and Blood of Christ be celebrated and distributed. This is true of the deacon, the sub-deacon and the lector, who proclaim the Word of God in readings from Scripture. Above all, it is true of the preacher and the celebrant. In the sermon, God Himself speaks to His people to-day; in the celebration of the Eucharist, Christ Himself is made present by the Holy Spirit, and He fulfils the memorial of His passion and resurrection.

When he says the eucharistic prayer, the celebrant is expressing the thanksgiving and intercession of the Church; but, above all, he is the instrument whereby Christ repeats the gestures and words of the Last Supper on the evening of the first Maundy Thursday. These gestures and these words effect the sacrament of the one and only sacrifice and of the real presence of Christ. And so the celebrant cannot be compared to the mediatorial priest of the Old Covenant. It is his function either to express the prayer of the Church or to be the sign and instrument of Christ, the High Priest, who comes to proclaim the Word of God in His Church, manifest His real presence in the sacrament, and present His one and only sacrifice in thanksgiving and intercession before the Father. The function of the celebrant is best symbolized when, at the beginning of the eucharistic prayer and at the invocation of the Holy Spirit (epiclesis), he raises his hands, as if offering them to God, so that He may fill them with His fullness; he is the instrument of Christ, who comes to accomplish the eucharistic memorial Himself.

In order to show that they are responsible for directing the liturgy, the officiants wear their white habit, and the stole of the seasonal liturgical colour (the altar frontal, chalice veil and other ornaments could be of the same symbolic colour).

At Taizé the Prior presides over the officiants in the liturgy. He gives the absolution at the introit, and benedictions in the name of the Lord before the Gospel and at the end of the Eucharist.

The shape of the liturgy

The eucharistic liturgy at Taizé is divided, following the Western use, into three parts :

> *the Introit Liturgy,*
>
> *the Liturgy of the Word,*
>
> *the Eucharistic Liturgy.*

The Introit Liturgy comprises preparation for celebration, and the entry into the presence of God; it is markedly escatological in character, because it is symbolic of our preparation for entry into the Kingdom of God, where the liturgy will be celebrated eternally.

The Liturgy of the Word comprises the reading, meditation and preaching of the Word of God; here the Prophets, the Apostles, Christ and the Church proclaim to us the good news of the Kingdom, and we respond with songs of acclamation and meditation.

The Eucharistic Liturgy comprises the Son's memorial of thanksgiving and intercession before the Father, celebrated sacramentally by the Church, which offers its poverty to God that He might fill it with His glory; it comprises also the communion of the Body and Blood of Christ, really present.

6

At Taizé the brothers of the community assemble in the common-room of the house, or in the sacristy for final preparation for the liturgy. They wear their white habits as a symbol of joy and praise, and of consecration to the service of God. The Prior announces further special intentions for intercession, and then gives the signal for the procession to move to the church door.

'Let us depart in peace!'

The brothers reply together: 'In the name of Christ. Amen.' They all follow him in order of seniority in the community; and when they reach the entrance to the church, they gather round the prior, who opens the door and begins the preparation.

1. *Repentance and pardon*

First the Prior, and then the community and the congregation confess their sins and ask for pardon. This is followed by the Calvinist solemn absolution. Before entering the church, which is a symbol of the Kingdom, the members of the community leave the burden of sin at the door, they disentangle themselves from all that binds them to the world, they leave behind them the preoccupations of the old man. That does not mean that, once inside the church they will forget the world, its difficulties and its sufferings; on the contrary, it is for the world that they will pray to the Lord. But though they will keep the world of men constantly present in their prayers throughout the liturgy, they leave the world of sin at the door, exorcizing it by confession and absolution.

The Prior at once places the celebration in the light of God the Holy Trinity, by the invocation of the Father and of the Son and of the Holy Spirit, and affirms that our only help is in the name of the Lord, the Creator of all things. That is why we dare to approach Him, to express our repentance in the confession of sins.

The confession is addressed to God, in the communion of saints. It is also addressed to the brethren in the faith, in order to ask their prayers. Sin endangers communion not only with God but also with the Church, and for that reason the confession

7

of sins is set within the communion of saints. In asking God for pardon, the community is asking for the renewal and strengthening of the bonds in which it is joined to all the saints in heaven and on earth and to the whole Church militant and triumphant. The sinner knows also that in his confession he is not alone; the universal brotherhood of Christians can be engaged in common intercession for pardon. This liturgical confession is to be distinguished from private confession, which it does not replace, because it is essentially the confession of the sins of the community in its service of Christ. Here each member acknowledges as his own the common failings in the obedience and ministry of all the people of God. Of course, each can confess his personal sin here, too; but that does not dispense him from having recourse to private confession and absolution for his faults. The remedy which is applied to the whole body of the repentant community should be completed by a remedy which is suitable for a particular member. Care must be taken of the general state of health, and also of the particular diseased member.

In the mutual request for pardon, absolution is conceived in eschatological terms; it is a stage in our journey towards the Kingdom: 'May the Almighty God have mercy upon thee, forgive thee thy sins, and bring thee to everlasting life.' Thus we go from pardon to pardon, from grace to grace, from absolution to absolution towards the Kingdom, which is coming and is everlasting life. The eschatological character of the eucharistic celebration throughout should be noted. The liturgy—in particular the Eucharist—is an anticipation of the Kingdom of God, a foretaste of Paradise, an opening onto heaven, indeed the joy of heaven on earth. The liturgy prepares us for the vision of God and for His praise in everlasting life.

Finally, in response to the confession of sins and the request for pardon, absolution is pronounced on all who repent and seek Jesus Christ for their salvation. The community and the congregation are now ready both to begin the liturgy and to enter the church, the symbol of the Kingdom of Heaven.

A beautiful sanctuary, lights, icons glorifying the work of Christ in image and colour, singing and organ music all join in

8

helping the created world to reflect something of the un-
imaginable splendour of the heavenly glory.

2. *Entry into the church (introit)*

The organist plays over the antiphon for the introit of the day,
which all then sing as they enter the nave. After each verse of
the psalm itself, the anthem is taken up as a refrain, expressing
the particular significance of the Sunday or of the festival which
is being celebrated. Every one goes to his place; and all sit to
finish the verses of the psalm, sung antiphonally by two choirs.
The introit ends with the trinitarian doxology, which is sung
standing, and then the antiphon is taken up for the last time.

3. *Supplication and praise (Kyrie and Gloria)*

The celebrant, accompanied by the deacon and sub-deacon, goes
and stands in front of the altar, and pronounces the Blessing of
the Kingdom (invocation) as in the Liturgy of St. John Chrysostom.
We will follow here one of three possible ways of beginning the
liturgy, the one which is most often used at Taizé. (The others
will be found in the text of the liturgy.) Again, the reference
to the Kingdom of God emphasizes the eschatological character
of the liturgy. The litany of the *Kyrie* and the *Gloria* follow immediately, exhibiting at the very beginning of the celebration
the two basic elements of prayer: supplication and praise, intercession and thanksgiving. The eucharistic prayer, the prayer *par
excellence*, will be essentially thanksgiving and intercession.

First, the litany enumerates intentions for the needs of the
Church and of the world. They are sung by the deacon or by a
cantor, interspersed with the words 'Kyrie eleison' and 'Christe
eleison.' The form of the litany is that of the Liturgy of St. John
Chrysostom; it helps us to realize more keenly our fellowship with
our Orthodox brethren. The short Greek supplications 'Kyrie
eleison . . . Christe eleison' come from the most ancient liturgies.
They express well the attitude of the Church at prayer, confessing
her poverty and humility and asking her Lord to come and hear
her prayers. 'Lord come, and have mercy.' It is the publican's
prayer, the true Christian prayer which expects everything from
God alone.

9

The Gloria, the dazzling hymn of praise, goes with the Kyrie and shows the other side of Christian prayer; after the humility of supplication, the joy of praise. The Gloria is an expanded version of the angelic hymn at Christmas. It exhausts the vocabulary of the worship of God; and it concludes the introit liturgy with an exultant cry, recalling in some respects the ecstatic utterances of glossolalia in the primitive Church. Seized by the Spirit, the Church seems unable to find sufficient human words to express the glory of the Lord.

4. Introit prayer (collect)

A short proper prayer closes the first part of the liturgy and opens the second. This is the introit prayer or 'collect' (collection, either of the faithful or of their intentions). Its concise form helps us to concentrate upon a simple intention. The deacon invokes a blessing on the congregation, whose prayer he is to express: 'The Lord be with you.' The members of the congregation return this greeting and benediction, thus recognizing that it is his function to put their prayer into words and speak it for them. These simple words of greeting and benediction express the priesthood of all the baptized—who in prayer have free access to God with no other mediator than Jesus Christ, but who at various moments in the liturgy entrust a minister with the expression of their worship, the saying of their prayer, the summing up here in the 'collect' (the introit prayer) of their special intention for the day. In some liturgies this mutual greeting and benediction occurs before every prayer, as a reminder that it is the royal priesthood of all the baptized, which is being expressed by the ministers. In the Taizé liturgy, these salutations have been strictly limited in order to avoid repetition; but whenever one of the ministers says a prayer, he tacitly receives this commission from the whole community of the baptized.

The prayer consists of four parts: The invocation of the name of God, sometimes with one or two attributes; the memorial, or recalling of some act of God on behalf of His people; the Church's particular intention for the day; and the conclusion, which is the recognition of Christ's unique mediation in the unity of the Trinity.

The whole congregation sings 'Amen' and affirms its participation in the prayer, its prayer, which it has commissioned the officiant to say on its behalf: 'Yes, that prayer is our prayer, and we want it to be answered.'

In the presence of her God, the Church now hears His Word in lections and preaching; and she responds with songs of acclamation and meditation.

1. *Prophecy and gradual*

The lector goes to the Bible, which is on the ambo; and, in the proclamation of an Old Testament lesson, the voice of the 'prophet' is heard. This is related to the gospel of the day. The threefold reading of prophecy, epistle and gospel is an ancient tradition. It occurs, for example, in the Ambrosian liturgy. Liturgiologists generally would like to recover it in churches which now have only the two New Testament lections.

The proclamation of the Word of God is introduced by an invocation of the Spirit of Truth, that He will lead the Church into all truth. This 'epiclesis' or invocation of the Holy Spirit upon the proclamation of the Word of God signifies that the Scriptures can be a dead letter to those who do not hear or read them in the light of the Holy Spirit. The Spirit vivifies the letter of Scripture, making it live and work effectively in the Church and in the hearts of the congregation. The Spirit will be invoked in the same way on two other occasions: before the offertory, the Spirit of Charity is invoked that He will fill with love the hearts of the faithful before they present their offerings at the altar; before the words of institution, the Creator Spirit is invoked to fulfil the word of the well-beloved Son, 'This is My Body . . . this is My Blood.' Without the Holy Spirit we are not able to join the offering of the Church to the unique sacrifice of Christ, we are not worthy to bring our offering to the altar; without the Holy Spirit, vivifying and actualizing the words of the Lord, the bread and the wine cannot become effectual

B

signs of the real presence of Christ. Thus the realism and the life of the liturgy depend upon the work of the Holy Spirit, whom the Church invokes: the Spirit of Truth upon the proclamation of the Word, the Spirit of Love upon the offering of the Church, the Creator Spirit upon the signs of the presence of Christ.

The Old Testament lesson is followed by the gradual, a hymn of meditation taken from the psalms. A cantor intones the antiphon, which is taken up by all; then he alone sings a verse of the psalm, and all take up the antiphon for the third time. This particular method of responsorial singing is very simple; it allows the whole congregation to sing the antiphons without elaborate rehearsal; its simplicity and the singing of the soloist are conducive to meditation after the lesson.

2. *Epistle and alleluia*

The prophet has spoken; now the apostle's voice will be heard. During the singing of the gradual the sub-deacon has replaced the lector, and he introduces the reading of the epistle of the day: 'Lord, sanctify us in the truth; Thy Word is truth.' Here, as in the Old Testament lesson, we are not hearing a man but the Word of God Himself. The reading, or rather the proclamation of the Word of God, is a 'mystery' in the Patristic sense of the word. God Himself works through the words which are spoken. He fills them with His Spirit, and enters the hearts of those who are well-disposed to receive these words, full of truth and of the life of God.

The response to the reading of the epistle is the acclamation, 'Alleluia.' This is at one and the same time an acclamation, a hymn of meditation and a processional. The alleluia has often been extended in traditional liturgical music to become a sort of ecstatic hymn, a kind of 'speaking in tongues.' The proper verse is taken from the psalms or from the New Testament, and it recalls the liturgical theme of the day. During the singing of the alleluia the sub-deacon, accompanied by two acolytes carrying candles and followed by the deacon, goes into the nave with the gospel-book. At Taizé this procession is given a symbolic meaning. The gospel is carried into the congregation, where it is to be proclaimed, as the Word made flesh came into the world to give it light.

3. *Gospel and hymn*

When the gospel is proclaimed, Christ Himself speaks. The deacon asks for the cleansing of his heart and lips, and requests the prior's blessing. He is to stand in the place of Christ, so that He can speak to the Church; he lends Him his voice, that the wisdom of Christ may be expressed. At Taizé, other brothers follow the French deacon and read the gospel in different languages, according to the needs of the congregation. In this way the universality of the gospel and of the Church is manifested.

The fact that the reading of the gospel is solemnized in this way does not imply that this text is 'the Word of God' to any greater extent than the epistle or the prophecy; but, since it contains Christ's own words, it helps us better to understand that in the proclamation of Scripture it is not a man, a prophet or an apostle who is speaking, but God Himself. The solemn form of the gospel gives to the reading of all Scripture its true worth and emphasizes liturgically its divine origin (*pars pro toto*).

The reading of the gospel is drawn out into meditation by the singing of a canticle, a Huguenot psalm, Lutheran chorale, or hymn after the gospel (Ambrosian *antiphona*).

4. *Sermon and meditation*

Now, after the prophet, the apostle and Christ, the Church's voice is heard preaching the Word of God. The sermon interprets and applies either one of the lections or another biblical text. A short period of silence gives an opportunity for private meditation and closes with the singing of another canticle.

This brings to an end the second part—the liturgy of the Word.

III. THE EUCHARISTIC LITURGY

The bread of the Word of God has been broken and shared at the 'evangelic table'; now the bread of the Body of Christ will be broken and shared at the 'eucharistic table.'

This part of the liturgy comprises three acts which are distinct but inseparable.

A. *Offertory*

B. *Thanksgiving*

C. *Communion*

Sanctified by the Word of God, the Church performs various acts of offering to her Lord: the offering of her faith, her prayer and her gifts—the outward signs of her inward offering and of her spiritual worship (Rom. 12: 1).

In this offering the Church realizes that she is nothing, and that in her Christ is all; she understands that her offering is of no worth unless it is the offering of Christ Himself. That is why the offertory leads into thanksgiving for the Lord's work of redemption: 'All things come of Thee, and our only offering is to recall Thy gifts and marvellous works.' The memorial of the Lord Himself will become the Church's only possible and valid offering—her true prayer of thanksgiving and intercession.

Finally, in order to show that the Church can give only what God first gives to her, Christ will become her nourishment in the communion of His Body and His Blood. The eucharistic Body feeds the ecclesiastical Body; the life of Christ vivifies the life of the Church; the Eucharist gathers the community together and gives it its shape; the Bread of Life nourishes the members of Christ for their sustenance unto life eternal and for their mission unto the ends of the earth.

A. *Offertory*

1. *of faith*. First the Church confesses her faith by saying the Nicene Creed or the Apostles' Creed: a résumé of the Word of God, which she has just heard. Her first act of offering is to proclaim her faith before God and men. Thus she demonstrates that the only thing in her which is good and to which she can witness, is a free gift of the Word of God.

The Christian is justified only before God by his faith, the gift of grace, which anticipates and gives rise to every genuinely spiritual impulse within him.

God, by His grace, gives faith; and He gives the words for expressing it: the Creed is the résumé of God's redemptive work, revealed in His Word.

2. *of prayer.* Faith leads to prayer; to love God is to love one's neighbour, showing one's love of God in the confession of faith leads to showing one's love of neighbour in intercessory prayer: *'credo ... memento ...* ; I believe in God ... remember, O Lord Thy servants and Thy handmaidens, and all men ...'

The prayer of intercession joins together the various memorials —of the Church, of the living, of saints, of the dead, of sinners, of unity and of the Kingdom. All the members and all the needs of the Church are presented to God by the deacon, expressing the prayer of the whole liturgical community. The celebrant or the deacon may add free intentions and the names of particular persons, committing them to 'Jesus Christ our High Priest'; for it is Christ who in the memorial of His sacrifice intercedes to the Father on our behalf. The Church prays in Him and through Him. Christ is like the High Priest in the Old Testament, who, when he came into the presence of Jehovah in the Holy of Holies, carried upon his breastplate precious stones, engraved with the names of the twelve tribes of Israel. At the Ascension our Lord entered the heavenly tabernacle, where now He offers us to the Father in living intercession. There to-day our prayer, like our faith, has no worth except in Him, and when it is taken by Him to the Father. Our intercession is answered in His name, in the name of His unique sacrifice and perpetual intercession. A new edition of the Taizé Eucharist will give variants for the prayer of intercession, and in particular the two litanies of the liturgy of the Church of South India.

3. *of gifts.* The intercession closes with, 'Maranatha, the Lord comes,' and the cantor intones the offertory antiphon, which all take up. Then he sings one or two verses of a psalm, alternating

with the antiphon. During the singing, the bread and wine and the offerings are brought to the altar. These gifts are material signs of the spiritual self-offering of the congregation. The Church, which has offered her faith and her prayer to God, now offers Him her whole being, to be sanctified by Him. This offering is a sign of love of God, and also a sign of love of neighbour. The material gifts will be used to alleviate the sufferings and the misery of men. *Liturgia* and *diaconia* are one. The spiritual worship, which is pleasing to God, is both the sacrifice of praising the Lord, and the sacrifice of helping men.

4. *offertory prayer.* The three ministers are now behind the altar, on which they have placed the eucharistic elements. With a short offertory prayer, the deacon both closes the act of offering of faith, prayer and gifts, and opens the second act of the eucharistic liturgy—thanksgiving.

This prayer expresses at one and the same time both the Church's desire and her incapability of offering anything of value. (Here there is a reversal of the situation.) Through Christ, the Church has offered her faith, her prayer and her gifts; but in doing this she has become aware of her poverty. Now the liturgy will make room for the memorial of Christ; Christ Himself, really present in accordance with His promise and word ('this is My Body . . . this is My Blood'), will take the place of the Church, and actualize His unique and perfect sacrifice. In this living memorial of His sacrifice the Lord takes all the members of the congregation (with Him and in Him) to present them to the Father for His blessing and to fill them with the power of His passion, of His resurrection and of the Holy Spirit.

B. *Thanksgiving*

This act of the liturgy is both thanksgiving (*action de grâce*) in the sense of the Church rendering praise to God for all His benefits, and also an action of grace, in the sense of God's work in the Church by the power of His grace. This is the moment when Christ and the Church are one in a perfect exchange of grace and praise. But all comes from God: 'All things come of Thee, and our only offering is to recall Thy gifts and marvellous works.'

1. *preface and Sanctus*. The celebrant salutes the Church and asks her assent to the praise, which he is to express on her behalf in the preface, the first stage of thanksgiving: 'The Lord be with you. . . . And with Thy spirit.' Then in the *Sursum Corda* he invites the Church to look only to God, and to give Him thanks. 'It is meet and right,' and so it is. Nothing here is now of any account but God, who gives grace to the Church in Christ and through the Holy Spirit, and whom the Church thanks in Christ and through the Holy Spirit.

The celebrant then begins to praise God in the words of the preface—which is proper to the liturgical season. At Taizé there are twenty-one proper prefaces for the liturgy. God's marvellous acts on behalf of His people are evoked in these praises, and they become the matter of the Church's thanksgiving. In accordance with the biblical way of prayer, it is in thanking God for His marvellous acts on behalf of His people that the Church receives present blessings, and is able to call upon the Holy Spirit to fulfil the mystery of the Eucharist and to make of bread and wine the sacrament of the Body and Blood of Christ.

In union with all the angelic powers and with the whole company of the saints, the Church concludes the preface with the trinitarian hymn *Sanctus*, 'Blessed be He that cometh in the name of the Lord.' Christ Himself now comes to function in the Eucharist; He takes the place of the celebrant to fulfil the memorial of His passion and resurrection. The celebrant is only the instrument of Christ's eucharistic action; he offers Him his hands and voice to perform the sacrament.

2. *epiclesis*. The celebrant effaces himself, so that through his voice and gestures may flow the voice and gestures of Christ. Now he is not only expressing the worship of the congregation, but he is also the sign and instrument of Christ the Priest, who presents the memorial of His sacrifice to the Father in the power of the Holy Spirit.

The prayer asks God to fill with His glory the Church's sacrifice of praise; to bless, to perfect and so to accept it; for this sacrifice of praise, symbolized by the bread and wine, now becomes the figure of the unique sacrifice of Christ. The Church's offering is effaced in the presence of the unique and perfect sacrifice of Christ.

This change can be produced only in the power of the Holy Spirit; and the prayer therefore invokes the Holy Spirit upon the Church and the Eucharist. The Holy Spirit will make the Church ready to enter humbly into the communion of the sacrifice of Christ, and to fall prostrate before the Cross, which is sacramentally present on the altar under the signs of bread and wine. The Holy Spirit will make the sacrament of the real presence of Christ, His Body and Blood, with bread and wine. He it is, the Holy Spirit the Creator, who consecrates the bread to be the Body of Christ and the wine to be the Blood of Christ, who vivifies, actualizes and fulfils the words, which the well-beloved Son spoke on the evening of the first Maundy Thursday. 'This is My Body . . . this is My Blood.'

In the Alexandrian tradition (Dêr-Balyzeh text) the epiclesis or invocation of the Spirit immediately precedes Christ's words of institution, uniting in a most happy way the work of the Holy Spirit and the work of Christ in the Eucharist. In the dialogue between East and West the action of the words of Christ has too often been set over against the action of the Holy Spirit; and the accent has been placed too exclusively upon consecration either by the words of Christ or by the Holy Spirit. This form of the liturgy of St. Mark is therefore of great ecumenical value: it unites in a single moment the work of the Spirit and the work of the Son in the Eucharist. The words of Christ are efficacious in the power of the Holy Spirit the Creator and Consecrator.

3. *institution*. The prayer recalls and actualizes the Lord's words at the Last Supper; and when he repeats these words the celebrant makes Christ's gestures, for the liturgy is celebrated as His memorial. It is no simple memory; the memorial is the actualization of the historical gestures of Christ, of the Last Supper and of the sacrifice of the Cross, which is presaged; the memorial is also a liturgical presentation to the Father of this, Christ's sacrifice, that He might receive it as the supreme prayer of the Church for the

faithful and for the world. The Body of Christ is indeed given for us, the faithful; the Blood of Christ is indeed the new covenant, the Blood poured out for many for the remission of sins. What Christ did once for all upon the Cross, He now makes present in His Church; and applies it to all who in faith receive it.

Thus, whenever the Eucharist is celebrated, the death of the Lord is proclaimed for the salvation of all who believe in Him, and the Church summons the Kingdom with her whole voice, 'until Christ come again.'

4. *memorial.* In celebrating the liturgy the Church participates in the mystery of Christ, made present in its fullness. The sacrament places the Church in the presence of the events of redemption; it makes her contemporaneous with the Cross; all that Christ has done for the salvation of the world is sacramentally present upon the altar, and the Church presents the Cross of Christ to the Father, as her supreme thanksgiving and intercession.

Christ is really present, and by Him the Church makes the memorial of the incarnation, passion, resurrection, ascension and intercession of the Lord. She relives these events, which are actualized by the real presence of Christ; she thanks God for them: and she commends herself to God by these marvellous acts of salvation asking Him to apply the power of sanctification by His Holy Spirit to her and to all men. This living memorial expresses both her fervent expectation of the return of Christ and her prayer for it; until He comes, the Church, in her celebration of the liturgy, begs the Lord insistently to establish His eternal and glorious Kingdom visibly at last.

This is perfect praise and supplication: to recall the gifts and marvellous works of God. The true prayer of the Church is Christ Himself.

That is why these eucharistic signs of the eternal sacrifice of Christ are the matter and the perfect form of His thanksgiving and intercession.

The Lord, who was pleased to accept the sacrifices of Abel, Abraham and Melchizedek, accepts the praises and prayers of the Church with goodwill, because they are the praises and prayers of Christ Himself; because she offers them to the Father in Christ; and because the Cross of Christ is her thanksgiving and intercession, the unique and perfect sacrifice, which she offers to the Father as her only recommendation.

5. *invocation.* The prayer continues with the request for the fruits of communion. At this point in the liturgy there is a new evocation of the role of the angels, who, according to the Book of Revelation, bring the prayers of the saints to God. The memorial of Christ is celebrated in Heaven in an angelic festival, of which our liturgy is an echo here below. And this memorial of the Lord, the Son's offering of praise and intercession to the Father in the unity of the Holy Spirit and the communion of the angels and saints, bears fruit—heavenly grace and blessing, richly poured out upon the Church by the Spirit in the communion of the Body and Blood of Christ.

6. *conclusion.* It is by Christ and in the Holy Spirit that the Father creates, sanctifies, quickens and blesses all the benefits He gives to us. There is nothing in this eucharistic prayer which is not done by the Son and the Spirit in communion with the Father. The eucharistic prayer is the Son's thanksgiving (*action de grâce*) to the Father in the power of the Holy Spirit; it is Christ's own action of grace—the act of worshipping the Father and of consecrating the eucharistic body and the ecclesiastical body by the Holy Spirit. It is indeed by Him, with Him and in Him—the Christ—that the Church offers her true spiritual worship to the Father in the unity of the Holy Spirit; by Him, for He is the intercessor who presents our prayer; with Him, for the matter of our praise and supplication is all that He has done for our salvation; in Him, for we achieve complete union with God in the communion of His Body and Blood. Our prayer passes through Him; our prayer is Him; our prayer is His life in us.

The congregation's 'Amen' affirms the Church's adherence to this great act of Christ—the Eucharist.[1]

[1] On weekdays a shorter eucharistic prayer replaces this one, which is reserved for Sundays and Festivals. Moreover, a future edition of the Eucharist at Taizé will also give the text of the eucharistic prayer of the liturgy of the Church of South India, as a mark of ecumenical fellowship.

c. *Communion*

The Eucharist is not only a mystery to be witnessed; it is also a sacrament to be received. The memorial of the redemptive work of the Lord now becomes our nourishment. The Church will communicate at the feast of the Body of Christ, really present in the Eucharist.

1. *Lord's prayer.* By the sacrifice of the Son we have become adopted sons of the Father and, strengthened by the Holy Spirit, we are bold to say the prayer of the children of God: Our Father. . . . This prayer is our spiritual preparation for communion. In particular, the request for daily bread reminds us that man does not live by bread alone, but by every word that proceeds from the mouth of God and by His very presence. As poor men we ask for the Bread of Life which is the Body and Blood of Christ.

2. *fraction, Agnus Dei and prayer of peace.* During the singing of the *Agnus Dei,* the hymn of our humble adoration of the Lamb 'who was slain,' the deacon and the sub-deacon break the eucharistic bread for the communion of the whole congregation. The hymn and the fraction have been prefaced by the words of St. Paul which give this act its special meaning. Although we are many, we form one body, because we all share in one bread. Thus we affirm that by our communion in the Body and Blood of Christ the Church is gathered together and built up in unity. The Eucharist is the sacrament which both creates and signifies unity.

The prayer for peace and unity in the Church is the ecumenical prayer *par excellence.* When we are gathered together by the Body of Christ, we ask the Lord to make real and visible the unity of all Christians, and to regard not the sin of the members but the faith of all. Separately the members can only foment division; united, they can move mountains by their faith.

3. *communion.* On the celebrant's invitation, the members of the congregation come forward to receive the Body and Blood of Christ. While they are gathering together the antiphon and proper verses of the communion hymn are sung. All say the prayer of

preparation together, while the celebrant communicates. He then gives communion to the deacon, the sub-deacon, and those who are to distribute it to the congregation.

Every one receives the Body and Blood of Christ, as the signs of His real presence, His death and resurrection. Taken separately the two eucharistic elements signify the separation of the Body and Blood of Christ upon the Cross, His sacrifice and painful death; but when they are re-united in each communicant they remind us that the Lord has come to life again, that He has been raised up. Thus by communion first in the Body and then in the Blood of Christ, every one participates in the redemptive power of the passion and resurrection of the Lord.

Then all go back to their places, taking up the antiphon and the verses of the communion hymn.

4. *thanksgiving and blessing*. The deacon says the third proper prayer in thanksgiving for the great benefits that have been received in the communion of the Body and Blood of Christ, really present in the Eucharist. This prayer both concludes the communion service and prepares us for daily witness and service, and for Christian life and love.

The Lord's blessing completes the liturgy; and there is now no reason to prolong it. The Christian community has received the blessing of Christ in His Body and Blood; now it must go out, realize His presence in life in the world and let it shine on all men. Christ will now come to men in the world by love and service. *Liturgia* and *diaconia* are one and the same reality. All men are close to the Church's heart in her liturgy, and the fullness of Christ which is received at the Eucharist is distributed to men by the Church and by each member in love and service.

Our liturgy and our service, our prayer and our word are one; this is Christ's work in us and through us for the salvation of all men.[1]

[1] For the underlying doctrine of the eucharistic liturgy please see: Max Thurian, *The Eucharistic Memorial, Part 2. The New Testament,* in Ecumenical Studies in Worship, Lutterworth Press, London, and John Knox Press, Richmond, U.S.A., 1960–1.

The ultimate reason for our belief in the real and living presence of Jesus Christ in the Eucharist is that He Himself, on the evening of Maundy Thursday, left us this sacrament of His presence and said: 'This is My Body . . . this is My Blood.'

The visible unity of all Christians in the one Church of Christ will be realized only when all Christians can communicate together at the same Eucharist. That means that faith in the real and living presence of Christ in the Eucharist is essential to the visible unity of Christians. The Eucharist is the sacrament of unity *par excellence.*

The real presence of Christ in the Eucharist is the presence of Christ crucified, risen and glorified, continuing His work of redemption in and through the Church. The real presence is not a static, immobile presence like that of an object, but the living presence of Jesus Christ, actualizing for us the mystery of redemption and His sacrifice made once for all upon the Cross. That is why we cannot speak of the real presence of Christ without speaking first of the presence of Christ's sacrifice in the Eucharist. The real presence is the real presence of Christ crucified and glorious, working in His Church by the ever-present power of His sacrifice.

From an ecumenical point of view, therefore, the Eucharist raises two questions, the solution of which by all would be a considerable advance towards unity:

   1. *In what sense is the eucharist a sacrifice?*

   2. *In what sense is Christ present in the Eucharist?*

In the course of history, theologians have given different answers to these questions. It is of cardinal importance that the ecumenical movement should help Christians to come to a common mind on the question of the Eucharist, because in the Eucharist the Church meets Christ concretely; she receives His Body and Blood; she deepens the quality of her life as the Body of Christ; and she prays for the return of Christ 'till He come.' The Eucharist is truly at the heart of the Church's life. And when Christians can communicate at the same altar there are no basic reasons why they should remain apart in separate communities.

1. *The Eucharist as sacrifice*

The primitive Church, faithful to the New Testament, saw in the Eucharist the new Passover meal of the New Covenant. As at the annual Passover meal the Jews actualized the deliverance of the People of God effected once at the Exodus from Egypt, so also in the eucharistic feast the Christians actualized the redemption of the People of God, effected once for all upon the Cross. In this mystery the Fathers of the Church saw a memorial, in the biblical sense of the word; that is to say, a liturgical act whereby *we bless God* for all His marvellous acts, and *remind Him* of what He has done previously, His mercy and His acts of blessing, in order that He should give to-day a further sign of His love. In this sense the Eucharist—the sacrament or actuality of the sacrifice of Christ—is a sacrifice of praise, which blesses God for His marvellous acts, and a sacrifice of supplication, which implores the Lord's grace. The Eucharist is a sacrifice of thanksgiving and a sacrifice of intercession.

Within the framework of the biblical concept of memorial, it is possible to call the Eucharist a sacrifice.

'The Eucharist is a sacrifice for three reasons:

'1. It is the sacramental *presence* of the sacrifice of the Cross, by the power of the Holy Spirit and the Word; and it is the liturgical *presentation* of the Son's sacrifice by the Church to the Father, in thanksgiving for all His blessings and in intercession that He may grant them afresh.

'2. It is the *participation* of the Church in the intercession of the Son before the Father in the Holy Spirit, that salvation may be accorded to all men, and that the Kingdom may come in glory.

'3. It is the *offering* which the Church makes of itself to the Father, united to the Son's intercession, as its supreme act of adoration and its perfect consecration in the Holy Spirit.' [1]

Without detracting at all from the uniqueness of the Cross, expiation, reconciliation and redemption, the Eucharist is the sacrament or the presence of the one and only sacrifice, the means whereby the application of salvation, communion with God and the intercession of Christ are continued in the Church

[1] *The Eucharist Memorial*, 2, p. 76.

to-day. The Eucharist is the Cross, present in the Church, extending the unique and perfect work of Christ to all men in space and time, and in depth. In the Eucharist the Church meets Christ, who applies salvation to all, deepens the communion of men with God, intercedes for all, and hastens the coming of the Kingdom.

2. *The real presence of Christ in the Eucharist*

The primitive Church understood Christ's words: 'This is My Body . . . this is My Blood' in a very simple way, which was both realistic and sacramental: realistic, because Christ spoke the truth, and He is really and concretely present in the Eucharist; sacramental, because His presence, unlike ours, is not carnal. In the Eucharist the glorious Christ is present, wholly and in person, in His Church, but in a sacramental and mysterious way. The view of the Fathers of the Church was that the bread and wine are changed into the Body and Blood of Christ, according to the mystery of God, who out of ordinary bread and wine makes the Body and Blood of Christ, the sacramental signs of His real presence. To-day, sharing their intention to be faithful and from an ecumenical point of view, we might sum up as follows our faith in the real presence of Christ in the Eucharist:

'1. The Body and Blood of Christ, His whole humanity and deity, are truly, really and substantially present in the Eucharist.

'This real presence of His Body and Blood is the presence of Christ crucified and glorified, here and now, under concrete signs. The meaning of every corporal presence is to attest that a person is concretely present and can enter into concrete communion. By the real presence of His Body and Blood, the Church knows that Christ is there concretely in the midst and it receives Him by means of a concrete sign. The substantial presence of Christ does not denote a material presence in the natural sense, but the presence of the profound reality of the Body and Blood of Christ crucified and glorified.

'2. Christ, then, through the Holy Spirit and His Word takes sovereign possession of the elements of bread and wine, draws them to Himself and assumes them into the fullness of His humanity and deity in such a way that they become truly, really and substantially His Body and Blood, according to the Gospel.

'The glorified Christ takes the bread and wine as a sign to manifest His corporal presence in the Church. The bread and wine of the Eucharist are no longer ordinary bread and wine. Of course their chemical nature remains that of bread and wine, but behind this faith must recognize the true and new substantial reality of the bread and wine: the Body and Blood of Christ. The Church believes that the bread and wine are the Body and Blood of Christ in the sense that the glorified Christ takes possession of them to make them a concrete sign of His presence in our midst (His eucharistic sign), a place where He may be found locally, contemplated sensibly and communicated concretely.

'3. The figure of the bread and the wine is the sign that Christ is our sustenance; this sign of bread and wine is the vehicle of the real presence of the Body and Blood of Christ in us. This real and corporal presence should be contemplated and received in the liturgical action when Christ acts with and for us and gives Himself to us in communion.

'The Eucharist is an action and an act of communion. The signs of bread and wine are eucharistized for the sacrifice of thanksgiving and intercession, which are accomplished in the communion.

'4. The Body and Blood of Christ, which are objectively present in the Eucharist for communion, really come to those who receive them: to those who have a right intention, as a means of sanctification, and to those who will not recognize the Body of Christ, through lack of faith, and the Body of the Church, through egotism, as a means of condemnation.

'St. Paul expressed the objectivity of the eucharistic presence of Christ when he pointed out the grave consequences of an unbelieving or egotistical act of communion, without discerning the Body of Christ or the Body of the Church by faith and love (1 Cor. 11: 27–34). Where there is an unworthy act of communion, he who lacks faith and love meets Christ, really present, but does not receive the fruits of this encounter: on the contrary he is condemned for lack of faith and love.

'5. Communion in the Body and Blood of Christ is at the same time a communion of each individual in the Body of Christ, the Church. United in Christ in one offering by the Church, the faithful are indissolubly joined together by communion in the Body of Christ.

'If the Church makes the Eucharist, the Eucharist makes the Church. The Eucharist unifies and joins together the members of the Body of Christ: those who have been baptized are joined together in unity and can but seek the deepening extension and fulfilment of their unity. As the sacrament of unity, the Eucharist is the sacrament of charity, which it supports and extends. . . . In the life of a local community the Eucharist is the place where the Church is built up and deepened in charity. That Church which celebrates the Eucharist frequently beholds Christ through the Eucharist, developing His charity, His unity, and making His word and His life effective in the world.' [1]

Separated Christians can have no greater desire for unity than that of being reunited one day in one and the same eucharistic faith at one and the same eucharistic communion, which will be the sign that their visible unity has been fully accomplished.

FRERE MAX THURION
sub-prior of the Taizé community

---

[1] *The Eucharistic Memorial*, pt. 2, pp. 120–4.

C

THE EUCHARISTIC LITURGY

SUNDAYS AND FESTIVALS

P : Prior (or his deputy)
C : Celebrant
D : Deacon
SD : Subdeacon
L : Lector
Ca : Cantor(s)
W : The whole community
V and R : Two parts of the community alternating

29

Introit

(Introit of the day: psalm and antiphon) [1]

Invocation

C   In the Name of the Father and of the Son and of the Holy
       Ghost. Amen.
       Our help is in the Name of the Lord.

W Who hath made heaven and earth. [2]

Confession

C   I confess to God Almighty,
       in the communion of the saints of heaven and of the earth,
       and to you my brethren,
       that I have sinned exceedingly in thought, word and deed:
       through my fault, my own fault, my own great fault;
       wherefore I beseech you, my brethren,
       in the communion of the saints of heaven and of the earth,
       to pray for me to the Lord our God.

W May the Almighty God have mercy upon thee,
       forgive thee thy sins,
       and bring thee to everlasting life.

C   Amen.

W I confess . . .

C   May the Almighty God have mercy upon you,
       forgive you your sins,
       and bring you to everlasting life.

W Amen.

[1] See the table of contents of GELINEAU'S *Fifty-three Psalms* (The Grail Press).

[2] On the First Sunday in Advent and the First Sunday in Lent the Ten Commandments (Exod. 20: 1–17) may be recited here.

30

Kyrie

W Lord, have mercy.
Christ, have mercy.
Lord, have mercy.

Absolution

C May each one of you acknowledge himself to be indeed a
sinner,
humbling himself before God,
and believe that it is the Father's will to have mercy upon
him in Jesus Christ;
to all who thus repent
and seek Jesus Christ for their salvation,
I declare the absolution of their sin
✝ in the name of the Father and of the Son and of the
Holy Ghost. Amen.

(The Gloria is then sung) [1]

---

[1] Except in Advent and Lent when the Collect follows immediately.

31

(on certain solemn festivals, as during the seasons of Christmas and Easter, the liturgy may be as follows)

Introit

Invocation

C   Blessed be the Kingdom of the Father and of the Son and of the Holy Ghost, now and for evermore, world without end.

W   Amen.

Litany of the Kyrie

(before saying . . . let us pray to the Lord, the deacon may add particular intentions)

D   In peace let us pray to the Lord . . .
For the peace that is from above and for the salvation of our lives . . .   let us pray to the Lord,

W   Kyrie eleison (Lord, have mercy)

D   For the peace of the whole world, the life of the Churches and their unity . . .   let us pray to the Lord,

W   Kyrie eleison (Lord, have mercy)

D   That we may celebrate the liturgy in the house of God with faith, fervour and obedience . . .   let us pray to the Lord,

W   Kyrie eleison (Lord, have mercy)

D   For the ministers of the Church and the whole company of faithful people . . .   let us pray to the Lord,

W   Christe eleison (Christ, have mercy)

D   For the governments of the nations, that they may ever be mindful of social justice and of the unity of mankind . . .
        let us pray to the Lord,

W   Christe eleison (Christ, have mercy)

D   For our community, our village (city), and our country, that the faith may there be renewed . . .
        let us pray to the Lord,

W Christe eleison (Christ, have mercy)

D For fair weather, abundant harvests and peaceful times . . .

let us pray to the Lord,

W Kyrie eleison (Lord, have mercy)

D For all who travel and are in danger, the sick, the afflicted, the prisoners, and that they all may be delivered . . .

let us pray to the Lord,

W Kyrie eleison (Lord, have mercy)

D That we may be freed from all tribulation, danger and necessity . . .   let us pray to the Lord,

W Kyrie eleison (Lord, have mercy)

(the Gloria is then sung)

(Or the invocation, confession and absolution could be said at the entrance to the church; and the introit sung in procession to the choir, followed by the litany and Gloria)

Gloria

(sung in chorus or antiphonally)

Glory be to God in highest heaven,

And on earth peace to men,

We praise Thee,

We bless Thee,

We worship Thee,

We glorify Thee,

We give thanks to Thee for Thy great glory

O Lord God, Heavenly King, God the Father Almighty.

O Lord, the only-begotten Son, Jesus Christ,

O Lord God, Lamb of God, Son of the Father,

Thou that takest away the sin of the world, have mercy upon us;

Thou that takest away the sin of the world, receive our prayer;

Thou that sittest at the right hand of the Father, have mercy upon

us.

For Thou only art holy,

Thou only art the Lord,

Thou only, O Christ,

With the Holy Ghost, art most high in the glory of God the

Father!

Amen.

Collect

D The Lord be with you.

W And with thy spirit.

D Let us pray (*Silence, followed by the collect of the day*)

W Amen.

34

Old Testament Lesson

SD or *L* Come, Holy Spirit of truth; lead us into all truth.
Old Testament Lesson from the book of . . .
or the Prophecy of . . .
(the reading of the day ending with Thanks be to God!)

Hymn of Meditation

(the gradual of the day [1] *sung responsorially)*

Ca (antiphon)
W (repetition of the antiphon)
Ca (verse)
W (repetition of the antiphon)

Epistle

SD Lord, sanctify us in the truth: Thy Word is truth.
. . . Epistle of St. . . . to . . .
or Lesson from the Acts of the Apostles.
or Lesson from the Revelation.
(the reading of the day ending with Glory be to Thee, O Lord!)

Alleluia

(the alleluia of the day sung responsorially)

Ca Alleluia.
W Alleluia.
Ca (verse)
W Alleluia.

(or tract of the day [2] *sung by a cantor)*

[1] In Eastertide: First Alleluia.

[2] Septuagesima, Lent and Passiontide.

35

Gospel

D Cleanse my heart and my lips, O God Almighty,
  who didst touch with a burning coal the lips of the
   prophet Isaiah;
  in Thy gracious mercy sanctify me,
  that I may faithfully proclaim Thy holy Gospel,
   through Christ our Lord, Amen.
  My brother, give me the blessing of the Lord.

P The Lord be in thy heart and on thy lips,
  that thou mayest joyfully proclaim His Gospel.

D Amen.

D Let us hear the Wisdom of Christ!
  The Gospel according to St. . . .

(the reading of the day, ending with Praise be to Thee, O Christ!*)*

Hymn after the Gospel

Sermon Silence Hymn

Creed

   The Apostles' Creed or the Nicene Creed

C Let us join together in brotherly love
  and with one heart and mind confess
  the faith of the universal Church:

W I believe in one God,
  the Father Almighty,
  Maker of heaven and earth,
  and of all things visible and invisible.

 I believe in one Lord, Jesus Christ,
  the only-begotten Son of God, begotten of His Father
   before all worlds:
  God of God, Light of Light,
  very God of very God,
  begotten not made, being of one substance with the
   Father, by whom all things were made.

36

Who for us men and for our salvation
   came down from Heaven;
   and was incarnate by the Holy Ghost of the Virgin Mary,
   and was made man;
   and was crucified also for us under Pontius Pilate;
   He suffered His passion and was placed in the tomb;
   the third day He rose again, according to the Scriptures;
   and ascended into Heaven and sitteth on the right hand of
      the Father;
   and He shall come again with glory to judge the living and
   the dead,
   whose Kingdom shall have no end.
I believe in the Holy Ghost,
   The Lord and giver of life,
   who proceedeth from the Father and the Son,
   who with the Father and the Son together is worshipped
      and glorified;
   who spake by the Prophets.
   I believe in one holy, catholic, and apostolic Church.
   I acknowledge one baptism for the remission of sins.
   And I look for the resurrection of the dead and the life of
      the world to come.
   Amen.

Intercession

C   Let us intercede before God.

D   Most merciful Father,
         we beseech Thee to accept our prayers and intercessions
            through Jesus Christ,
         Thy Son, our Lord.

W   O Lord, hear our prayer.

Memorial of the Church

D We offer first our prayers
  for Thy holy, universal Church;
  be pleased throughout the world to grant her peace,
  to guard, unite and govern her;
  we pray Thee also for all who are set in authority over
   her . . .
  and for all who, faithful to true doctrine,
  keep the christian, apostolic faith.

W O Lord, hear our prayer.

Memorial of the Living

D Remember O Lord,
  Thy servants and Thy handmaidens,
  and all who are round about us,
  whose faith Thou knowest, whose devotion Thou hast
   proved;
  this sacrifice of praise with them we offer unto Thee,
  the eternal, living and true God,
  and we address to Thee our prayers for all men . . .
  for the redemption of their lives,
  and for their hope of liberation and of peace.

W O Lord, hear our prayer.

Memorial of the Saints

D   United in one communion . . .
    (interpolation proper to certain festivals and their octave;
                            see page 41)

        we commemorate before Thee*
        (and) Thy blessed Apostles and Martyrs . . . .**
        and all the Saints . . . .;
        united with their faith, their lives and their prayer,
        we beseech Thee to grant unto us at all times
        the help of Thy strength and of Thy protection.

W   O Lord, hear our prayer.

Memorial of the Dead

D   We also commemorate, O Lord,
        Thy servants and Thy handmaidens,
        who have gone before us with the sign of faith,
        and are at peace . . .
        To all who rest in Christ, Thou grantest, Lord,
        the place of refreshment, light and peace.

W   O Lord, hear our prayer.

---

    * the Blessed Virgin Mary,
      Mother of our God and Lord Jesus Christ,
      moreover we commemorate
      Saint John the Baptist, the Forerunner

    ** Peter and Paul, Andrew, James, John, Thomas,
      James, Philip, Bartholomew, Matthew, Simon and Jude,
      Stephen, Matthias and Barnabas . . .

Memorial of Sinners

D To us sinners also, Thy servants,
who put our trust in Thine infinite mercy,
grant a place in the community
of Thy holy Apostles and Martyrs and of all the Saints;
into whose company admit us,
not weighing our merit,
but amply pardoning us.

W O Lord, hear our prayer.

Memorial of Unity

D As the bread which shall be broken,
was once scattered on the mountains,
and being gathered together became one,
so gather Thy Church together,
from the ends of the earth into Thy Kingdom.

W O Lord, hear our prayer.

Free Prayers

. . . through our High Priest, Jesus Christ.
W O Lord, hear our prayer.

Memorial of the Kingdom

D Come, Holy Spirit of charity
fill the hearts of Thy faithful people,
and kindle in them the fire of Thy love;
come, Lord Jesus, come quickly.

W Maranatha, the Lord cometh.

Christmas

. . . and celebrating (the most sacred night) the most sacred day,
whereon the Blessed Virgin Mary
brought forth the Saviour of our world,
we commemorate before Thee
the Mother of our God and Lord Jesus Christ;
moreover we commemorate
Saint John the Baptist, the Forerunner,
and Thy blessed Apostles and Martyrs . . .

Epiphany

. . . and celebrating the most sacred day,
whereon Thine only-begotten Son, who shareth Thine eternity and glory
was visibly manifested with His body
in the reality of our human flesh,
we commemorate before Thee . . .

Easter

. . . and celebrating (the most sacred night) the most sacred day
of the Resurrection of our Lord Jesus Christ
in His human nature,
we commemorate before Thee . . .

Ascension

. . . and celebrating the most sacred day,
whereon Thine only-begotten Son, our Lord,
our corruptible nature united to Himself,
sat down at the right-hand of Thy glory,
we commemorate before Thee . . .

Pentecost

. . . and celebrating the most sacred day of Pentecost,
whereon the Holy Spirit appeared to the Apostles
in countless tongues of fire,
we commemorate before Thee . . .

Litany

D In peace let us pray to the Lord . . .
For the peace that is from above and for the salvation of our lives . . .   let us pray to the Lord.

W O Lord, hear our prayer.

D For the peace of the whole world, the life of the churches and their unity . . .   let us pray to the Lord.

W O Lord, hear our prayer.

D That we may celebrate the liturgy in the house of God with faith, fervour and obedience . . .   let us pray to the Lord.

W O Lord, hear our prayer.

D For the ministers of the Church and the whole company of faithful people . . .   let us pray to the Lord.

W O Lord, hear our prayer.

D For the governments of the nations, that they may ever be mindful of social justice and of the unity of mankind . . .
let us pray to the Lord.

W O Lord, hear our prayer.

D For our community, our village (city) and our country, that the faith there may be renewed . . .   let us pray to the Lord.

W O Lord, hear our prayer.

D For fair weather, abundant harvests and peaceful times . . .
let us pray to the Lord.

W O Lord, hear our prayer.

D For all who travel and are in danger, the sick, the afflicted, the prisoners, and that they all may be delivered . . .
let us pray to the Lord.

W O Lord, hear our prayer.

D That we may be freed from all tribulation, danger and necessity . . .   let us pray to the Lord.

W O Lord, hear our prayer.

(free prayers)

... through our High Priest, Jesus Christ.

W O Lord, hear our prayer.

D Come Holy Spirit of charity,
     fill the hearts of Thy faithful people,
     and kindle in them the fire of Thy love;
     come Lord Jesus, come quickly.

W Maranatha, the Lord cometh.

OR, particularly when the litany has been said at the beginning:

Memento

D In peace let us pray to the Lord ...
  Let us ask of the Lord peace in the Church,
     and for each one of us the grace of a holy life;

W O Lord, hear our prayer.

D Let us ask of the Lord brotherly love
     by the help of His Holy Spirit.

W O Lord, hear our prayer.

D Let us commit ourselves and each other to our God.

W O Lord, hear our prayer.

D Let us commemorate before the Lord
     all who have left this world and have died in the faith ...
     May God bestow on them the crown of life in the day of
       resurrection
     and judge them worthy with the righteous who have
       pleased Him
     to enter into the joy of their Master.

W O Lord, hear our prayer.

D Let us recall before the Lord all His servants and witnesses
     in times past,
     particularly Abraham, the father of all believers,
     Moses, Samuel and David, Elijah, Isaiah, Jeremiah and all
      the prophets,

43

D

John the Baptist, the Forerunner,
Peter and Paul, John and James and the other apostles,
Stephen the first martyr,
Mary the Mother of the Lord,
And all the saints, martyrs and doctors of the Church,
in every age and in every land.

W O Lord, hear our prayer.

D May the Lord God, in His mercy
give us with them hope in His salvation
and in the promise of eternal life in His Kingdom.

W O Lord, hear our prayer.

(free prayers)

. . . through Jesus Christ, our High Priest.

W O Lord, hear our prayer.

D Come Holy Spirit of charity,
fill the hearts of Thy faithful people,
and kindle in them the fire of Thy love;
come Lord Jesus, come quickly.

W Maranatha, the Lord cometh.

Offertory hymn

*(offertory of the day; antiphon and verses of a psalm if there be
one, sung as at the gradual)* [1]

Offertory prayer

D Let us pray *(silence, followed by the offertory prayer of the
day)*

W Amen.

---

[1] During this hymn the bread and wine and offerings are brought to the altar;
or the bread and wine, if already on the altar, are uncovered.

Eucharistic prayer

Dialogue

C   The Lord be with you.

W   And with thy spirit.

C   Lift up your hearts.

W   We lift them up unto the Lord.

C   Let us give thanks unto our Lord God.

W   It is meet and right so to do.

Preface

C   *(preface of the day, see pages 67 to 85)*

Sanctus

W   Holy, Holy, Holy,
Lord God of hosts,
Heaven and earth are full of Thy glory.
Hosanna in the highest.
Blessed be He that cometh in the name of the Lord.
Hosanna in the highest.

45

†

Epiclesis

OUR FATHER, GOD OF THE HOSTS OF HEAVEN
FILL WITH THY GLORY
THIS OUR SACRIFICE OF PRAISE.

†

BLESS, PERFECT AND ACCEPT
THIS OFFERING
AS THE FIGURE
OF THE ONE AND ONLY SACRIFICE OF OUR LORD.

†

SEND THY HOLY SPIRIT
UPON US AND OUR EUCHARIST:
CONSECRATE THIS BREAD TO BE THE BODY OF CHRIST
AND THIS CUP TO BE THE BLOOD OF CHRIST;
THAT THE CREATOR SPIRIT
MAY FULFIL THE WORD OF THY WELL-BELOVED SON.

Institution

WHO, IN THE SAME NIGHT THAT HE WAS BETRAYED
TOOK BREAD
AND, WHEN HE HAD GIVEN THANKS, BRAKE IT
AND GAVE IT TO HIS DISCIPLES, SAYING:
TAKE, EAT,
THIS IS MY BODY WHICH IS GIVEN FOR YOU;
DO THIS AS THE MEMORIAL OF ME.

LIKEWISE, AFTER SUPPER
HE TOOK THE CUP
AND, WHEN HE HAD GIVEN THANKS,
HE GAVE IT TO HIS DISCIPLES, SAYING:
DRINK YE ALL OF THIS,
FOR THIS CUP IS THE NEW COVENANT
IN MY BLOOD
WHICH IS SHED FOR YOU AND FOR MANY
FOR THE REMISSION OF SINS;
WHENEVER YE DRINK IT,
DO THIS AS THE MEMORIAL OF ME.

✝

WHENEVER
WE EAT THIS BREAD
AND DRINK THIS CUP,
WE PROCLAIM THE LORD'S DEATH
TILL HE COME.

Memorial

WHEREFORE, O LORD,
WE MAKE BEFORE THEE
THE MEMORIAL OF THE INCARNATION
AND THE PASSION OF THY SON,
HIS RESURRECTION FROM HIS SOJOURN WITH THE
DEAD,
HIS ASCENSION INTO GLORY IN THE HEAVENS,
HIS PERPETUAL INTERCESSION
FOR US;
WE AWAIT AND PRAY FOR HIS RETURN.

47

✝

ALL THINGS COME OF THEE AND OUR ONLY
OFFERING
IS TO RECALL THY GIFTS AND MARVELLOUS WORKS.

✝

MOREOVER WE PRESENT TO THEE, O LORD OF GLORY
AS OUR THANKSGIVING
AND INTERCESSION
THE SIGNS OF THE ETERNAL SACRIFICE OF CHRIST,
UNIQUE AND PERFECT, LIVING AND HOLY
THE BREAD OF LIFE WHICH COMETH DOWN FROM
HEAVEN
AND THE CUP OF THE FEAST IN THY KINGDOM.

✝

IN THY LOVE AND MERCY
ACCEPT OUR PRAISE AND OUR PRAYERS
IN CHRIST,
AS THOU WAST PLEASED TO ACCEPT
THE GIFTS OF THY SERVANT ABEL THE RIGHTEOUS,
THE SACRIFICES OF OUR FATHER ABRAHAM,
AND OF MELCHIZEDEK,
THY HIGH PRIEST.

48

ALMIGHTY GOD, WE BESEECH THEE
THAT THIS PRAYER MAY BE BORNE
BY THE HANDS OF THINE ANGEL
TO THY ALTAR IN THY PRESENCE ON HIGH;
AND WHEN WE RECEIVE,
COMMUNICATING AT THIS TABLE,
THE BODY AND BLOOD OF THY SON,
MAY WE BE FILLED WITH THE HOLY SPIRIT
AND ENDOWED WITH GRACE
AND HEAVENLY BLESSINGS,
THROUGH CHRIST OUR SAVIOUR.

Conclusion

BY WHOM, O LORD
THOU EVER DOST CREATE, SANCTIFY, QUICKEN,
BLESS AND GIVE US ALL THY BENEFITS.

✝

BY WHOM,
AND WITH WHOM,
AND IN WHOM,
BE UNTO THEE,
O FATHER ALMIGHTY,
IN THE UNITY OF THE HOLY SPIRIT,
ALL HONOUR AND GLORY,
WORLD WITHOUT END.

℣   AMEN.

Lord's Prayer

C Enlightened by the Saviour's precept,
       and taught by His commandment, we are bold to say:
           Our Father, which art in Heaven,
               hallowed be Thy Name,
                   Thy Kingdom come,
       Thy will be done in earth as it is in Heaven,
               Give us this day our daily bread,
                   And forgive us our trespasses
           As we forgive them that trespass against us.
               Lead us not into temptation,
                   but deliver us from evil.
       For Thine is the Kingdom, the power and the glory,
                   for ever and ever.
                       Amen.

Fraction

C The bread which we break
       is the communion of the Body of Christ.
   The cup of blessing for which we give thanks
       is the communion of the Blood of Christ.
       Since there is but one bread,
       we who are many form one body,
       for we all share in this one bread.

Agnus Dei

W O Lamb of God, that takest away the sin of the world,
       have mercy upon us!
   O Lamb of God, that takest away the sin of the world,
       have mercy upon us!
   O Lamb of God, that takest away the sin of the world,
       grant us Thy peace!

50

Kiss of peace

C O Lord Jesus Christ, who didst say to Thine apostles:
      Peace I leave with you,
      My peace I give unto you,
      Regard not my sins but the faith of Thy Church;
      according to Thy will, grant her peace,
      and gather her into unity,
      for Thou livest and reignest world without end. Amen.
    Peace be with thee.

D And with thy spirit.
*(the kiss of peace goes from the celebrant to the deacon, then to the
sub-deacon and from him to the community and to the congrega-*
tion)

Invitation

C Holy things for the holy.

W One only is holy, one only is the Lord:
      Jesus Christ, to the glory of God the Father.

C Taste and see how gracious the Lord is.
      Come, for all is prepared.

Communion hymn

*(communion hymn of the day: antiphon and verses of a psalm, if
there be one, sung as at the gradual)*

Communion

W I will receive the Bread of Heaven and call upon the name
      of the Lord:
      Lord, I am not worthy that Thou shouldest come under
      my roof,
      but speak one word only and I shall be healed.
      May the Body of our Lord Jesus Christ
      preserve my life unto eternity!

        (the celebrant communicates)

What reward shall I give unto the Lord for all the benefits
He hath done unto me?
I will raise the cup of salvation and call upon the name of
the Lord.
I will cry out: Praised be the Lord,
and I shall be delivered from mine enemies.
May the Blood of our Lord Jesus Christ
preserve my life unto eternity.

*(the celebrant gives communion to the officiants, saying to the
deacon:)*

C The Body of Christ.
The Blood of Christ, the cup of Life.

*(the deacon and the sub-deacon and other officiants, if there
be any such, give communion to the community and to the
congregation; the deacon begins by saying:)*

D Behold the Lamb of God, which taketh away the sin of the
world.

(at the end the celebrant says:)

C Depart in peace!
*(each goes back to his place, taking up the communion hymn,
if there be one: the antiphon and other verses of the psalm)*

Prayer of thanksgiving

D Let us pray *(silence, followed by post-communion of the day)*
W Amen.

Blessing

D Let us bless the Lord.
W Thanks be to God.
C or P May God Almighty,
the Father, the Son and the Holy Ghost, bless you.
W Amen.

WEEKDAYS

(the introit of the day may be sung: psalm and antiphon)

Invocation

C   In the Name of the Father and of the Son and of the Holy
Ghost. Amen.

I will go unto the altar of God.

W   Even unto the God of my joy and gladness.

C   Our help is in the Name of the Lord.

W   Who hath made heaven and earth.

Confession

C   I confess to God Almighty,
in the communion of the saints
of Heaven and of the earth,
and to you my brethren,
that I have sinned exceedingly in thought, word and deed :
through my fault, my own fault, my own great fault;
wherefore I beseech you, my brethren,
in the communion of the saints of heaven and of the earth,
to pray for me to the Lord our God.

W   May the Almighty God have mercy upon thee,
forgive thee thy sins,
and bring thee to everlasting life,

C   Amen.

W   I confess . . .

C   May the Almighty God have mercy upon you,
forgive you your sins,
and bring you to everlasting life.

W   Amen.

(here the celebrant may read the introit of the day: antiphon, verse,
doxology,[1] antiphon, if it has not been sung at the beginning.
the liturgy could also begin here with the singing or reading of the
introit, omitting the confession, and proceeding directly to the
collect)

---

[1] C Glory be to the Father and to the Son and to the Holy Ghost.
W As it was in the beginning, is now and ever shall be, world without end.
Amen.

Collect

C The Lord be with you.

W And with thy spirit.

C Let us pray *(silence, followed by the collect of the day)*

W Amen.

*Old Testament Lesson
or Epistle*

> *(the reading of the day, introduced by the name of the book)*
> Thanks be to God.
>
> *(the gradual and alleluia, or the tract of the day, may be
> read by the celebrant, or sung)*

Gospel

> *(the reading of the day, introduced by the name of the
> book only)*
> Praise be to Thee, O Christ.

Sung response

Intercession

C Remember O Lord, Thy servants and Thy handmaidens . . .
>> and all who are round about us;
>> whose faith Thou knowest, whose devotion Thou hast
>> proved;
>> this sacrifice of praise with them we offer unto Thee,
>> the eternal, true and living God,
>> and we address to Thee our prayers for all men . . .
>> for the redemption of their lives,
>> and for their hope of liberation and of peace,
>> through Christ, our Lord.

W Amen.

Offertory Antiphon

(the offertory of the day is read by the celebrant, or sung; he uncovers the bread and the cup)

Offertory prayer

C Let us pray *(silence, followed by the offertory prayer of the day)*

W Amen.

Eucharistic prayer

Dialogue

C   The Lord be with you.

W   And with thy spirit.

C   Lift up your hearts.

W   We lift them up unto the Lord.

C   Let us give thanks unto our Lord God.

W   It is meet and right so to do.

C   *(preface of the day, or common)*

Preface

IT IS TRULY MEET AND RIGHT,

OUR JOY AND OUR SALVATION,

THAT WE SHOULD AT ALL TIMES AND IN ALL PLACES

GIVE THANKS UNTO THEE

O LORD, HOLY FATHER,

ALMIGHTY, EVERLASTING GOD,

THROUGH CHRIST OUR LORD.

(free thanksgiving may be made here)

BY WHOM THE ANGELS PRAISE THY MAJESTY,

DOMINIONS WORSHIP THEE

AND POWERS STAND IN AWE;

THE HEAVENS AND THE HEAVENLY HOSTS

AND THE BLESSED SERAPHIM

UNITED IN ONE JOY, EXTOL THEE;

WITH WHOSE SONGS, WE PRAY THEE, JOIN OUR VOICES

IN ONE PROCLAMATION OF THY PRAISE:

57

Sanctus

W Holy, Holy, Holy,
      Lord God of hosts,
      Heaven and earth are full of Thy glory.
      Hosanna in the highest.
      Blessed be He that cometh in the name of the Lord.
      Hosanna in the highest.

Epiclesis

OUR FATHER, GOD OF THE HOSTS OF HEAVEN,
THOU ART HOLY AND THY GLORY KNOWETH NO
BOUNDS.

✝

SEND THY HOLY SPIRIT
UPON US AND OUR EUCHARIST:
CONSECRATE THIS BREAD TO BE THE BODY OF CHRIST
AND THIS CUP TO BE THE BLOOD OF CHRIST;
THAT THE CREATOR SPIRIT
MAY FULFIL THE WORD OF THY WELL-BELOVED SON.

Institution

WHO, IN THE SAME NIGHT THAT HE WAS BETRAYED,
TOOK BREAD
AND, WHEN HE HAD GIVEN THANKS, BRAKE IT
AND GAVE IT TO HIS DISCIPLES, SAYING:
TAKE, EAT,
THIS IS MY BODY WHICH IS GIVEN FOR YOU;
DO THIS AS THE MEMORIAL OF ME.
LIKEWISE, AFTER SUPPER
HE TOOK THE CUP

AND, WHEN HE HAD GIVEN THANKS,
HE GAVE IT TO HIS DISCIPLES, SAYING:
DRINK YE ALL OF THIS,
FOR THIS CUP IS THE NEW COVENANT
IN MY BLOOD
WHICH IS SHED FOR YOU AND FOR MANY
FOR THE REMISSION OF SINS;
WHENEVER YE DRINK IT,
DO THIS AS THE MEMORIAL OF ME.

✝

WHENEVER
WE EAT THIS BREAD
AND DRINK THIS CUP,
WE PROCLAIM THE LORD'S DEATH
TILL HE COME.

Memorial

WHEREFORE, O LORD,
WE MAKE BEFORE THEE
THE MEMORIAL OF THE INCARNATION
AND THE PASSION OF THY SON,
HIS RESURRECTION FROM HIS SOJOURN WITH
THE DEAD,
HIS ASCENSION INTO GLORY IN THE HEAVENS,
HIS PERPETUAL INTERCESSION
FOR US;
WE AWAIT AND PRAY FOR HIS RETURN.

59

E

†

MOREOVER, WE PRESENT TO THEE, LORD OF GLORY
AS OUR THANKSGIVING
AND INTERCESSION,
THE SIGNS OF THE ETERNAL SACRIFICE OF CHRIST,
UNIQUE AND PERFECT, LIVING AND HOLY,
THE BREAD OF LIFE WHICH COMETH DOWN FROM
HEAVEN
AND THE CUP OF THE FEAST IN THY KINGDOM.

Invocation

GRANT US THE POWER OF THE HOLY SPIRIT,
THAT WE MAY DISCERN THE BODY AND THE BLOOD
OF CHRIST . . .
MAY THIS COMMUNION TRANSFORM OUR LIVES,
TAKE AWAY OUR SINS,
FILL OUR HEARTS WITH THE HOLY SPIRIT,
GIVE US THE FULLNESS
OF THE KINGDOM OF HEAVEN
AND CONFIDENCE BEFORE THEE,
AND DELIVER US FROM ALL CONDEMNATION,
THROUGH CHRIST OUR SAVIOUR.

Conclusion

BY WHOM, O LORD
THOU EVER DOST CREATE, SANCTIFY, QUICKEN,
BLESS AND GIVE US ALL THY BENEFITS.

✝

BY WHOM,
AND WITH WHOM,
AND IN WHOM,
BE UNTO THEE,
O FATHER ALMIGHTY,
IN THE UNITY OF THE HOLY SPIRIT,
ALL HONOUR AND GLORY,
WORLD WITHOUT END.

W AMEN.

Aariable Invocations

(the invocation, from 'May this communion . . .' may be replaced by one of the following: for a daily eucharist, they should be taken in succession and varied each day; the last but one should be kept for festivals of saints, and the last for festivals of martyrs)

. . . Gather into unity all who partake of this holy communion, fill them with the Holy Spirit, and strengthen their faith in the truth; so shall we be enabled to praise Thee and glorify Thee, through Thy well-beloved Son, Christ, our Saviour. By whom, O Lord . . .

. . . May all who are partakers of this holy communion be strengthened in the faith, find remission of their sins, be delivered from the snare of the Devil, be filled with the Holy Spirit, the witness of the sufferings of the Lord Jesus, be made worthy of Thy Son, and obtain with Thy reconciliation, O Almighty Master, eternal life, through Christ, our Lord. By whom . . .

. . . May He come among us and sanctify all things, the Holy Spirit, the Lord, who giveth life and who reigneth with Thee, O God and Father and with Thy well-beloved Son; who spake by the Law, the Prophets and the New Testament; who at the River Jordan appeared like a dove upon our Lord Jesus Christ and remained on Him; who in Jerusalem on the day of Pentecost came down in the likeness of tongues of fire upon the Holy Apostles; may He prepare in us the coming of Thy Christ, our Saviour. By whom, O Lord . . .

. . . May all who are partakers of this holy communion obtain life and resurrection, remission of sins, health of body and soul, illumination of mind, and assurance in the last judgment of Thy Christ, our Saviour. By . . .

. . . Strengthen and increase in us the faith, the hopes of eternal life to come, and the love of the children of God, through Christ, our Saviour. By whom . . .

. . . Grant that all we, who share one bread and one cup, may be united with each other in the communion of the one Holy Spirit; and may none of us partake of the Body and the Blood of Thy Son unto judgment and condemnation; but may we find

mercy and grace with all the saints who from the beginning have
been pleasing unto Thee; and grant us with one heart and voice to
glorify and praise Thy Holy Name, through Christ our Saviour;
By whom, O Lord . . .

. . . May He bring to us remission of sins, the great hope of
the resurrection from the dead, and the new life in the Kingdom
of Heaven with those who were pleasing unto Thee, through
Christ our Saviour. Through whom . . .

Lord's Prayer

C Enlightened by the Saviour's precept,
        and taught by His commandment, we are bold to say:
                Our Father, which art in Heaven,
                        hallowed be Thy Name,
                        Thy Kingdom come,
            Thy will be done in earth as it is in Heaven.
                Give us this day our daily bread,
                    and forgive us our trespasses
            as we forgive them that trespass against us.
                    Lead us not into temptation
                        but deliver us from evil.
        For Thine is the Kingdom, the power and the glory,
                        for ever and ever.
                            Amen.

Fraction

C The bread which we break
  is the communion of the Body of Christ.
 The cup of blessing for which we give thanks
  is the communion of the Blood of Christ.
  Since there is but one bread,
  we who are many form one body,
  for we all share in this one bread.

Agnus Dei

W O Lamb of God, that takest away the sin of the world,
  have mercy upon us!
  O Lamb of God, that takest away the sin of the world,
  have mercy upon us!
  O Lamb of God, that takest away the sin of the world,
  grant us Thy peace!

Prayer for peace

C O Lord Jesus Christ, who didst say to Thine apostles:
  Peace I leave with you,
  My peace I give unto you.
  Regard not my sins but the faith of Thy Church;
  according to Thy will, grant her peace,
  and gather her into unity,
  for Thou livest and reignest world without end. Amen.

Invitation

C Come, for all is prepared.

Communion Antiphon

(the communion of the day is read by the celebrant; or it is sung)

Communion

W I will receive the Bread of Heaven and call upon the name of
the Lord:
Lord, I am not worthy that Thou shouldest come under
my roof,
but speak one word only and I shall be healed.
May the Body of our Lord Jesus Christ
preserve my life unto eternity!
(the celebrant communicates)
What reward shall I give unto the Lord for all the benefits He
hath done unto me?
I will raise the cup of salvation and call upon the name of
the Lord.
I will cry out: Praised be the Lord,
and I shall be delivered from mine enemies.
May the Blood of our Lord Jesus Christ
preserve my life unto eternity.
*(the celebrant and other officiants, if there be any such, give
communion to the community and to the congregation; the
celebrant begins by saying:)*
C Behold the Lamb of God, which taketh away the sin of the
world.
(at the end the celebrant says:)
C Depart in peace.

Prayer of thanksgiving

C Let us pray *(silence, followed by post-communion of the day)*
W Amen.

Blessing

C   Let us bless the Lord.

W   Thanks be to God.

C or P   May God Almighty,
       the Father, the Son and the Holy Ghost, bless you.

W   Amen.

Preface of Advent:	every day from the First Sunday in Advent until Christmas Eve (24th December).
Preface of Christmas:	every day from Christmas night until the eve of the Epiphany (5th January).
Preface of Epiphany:	every day from the Epiphany until the eve of the Baptism of Christ (12th January).
Preface of the Baptism:	the Baptism of Christ and Sundays after Epiphany.
Common Preface:	weekdays after Epiphany until the beginning of Lent.
Preface of the Trinity:	Sundays called Septuagesima, Sexagesima and Quinquagesima.
Prefaces of Lent:	one for Sundays and one for weekdays.
Preface of the Passion:	from Passion Sunday until Good Friday, except Palm Sunday and Maundy Thursday.

Preface of Palm Sunday—Preface of Maundy Thursday.

Preface of Easter:	every day from Easter Eve until the eve of the Ascension.
Preface of the Ascension:	every day from the Ascension until the eve of Pentecost.
Preface of Pentecost:	every day from Pentecost until the eve of Trinity Sunday.
Preface of the Trinity:	Sundays from Trinity Sunday until the feast of Saints Peter and Paul (29th June).
Common Preface:	weekdays from Pentecost to Advent.
Preface of the Church:	Sundays from the feast of Saints Peter and Paul until the Transfiguration (6th August).

Preface of the Kingdom:	Sundays from the Transfiguration until Michaelmas Day (29th September).
Preface of Unity:	Sundays from Michaelmas Day until the Feast of Christ the King (last Sunday in October); every day during the Week of Prayer for Christian Unity (18th–25th January).
Preface of Christ the King:	Sundays from the Feast of Christ the King until the last Sunday after Pentecost.

Preface of the Virgin Mary.

Preface of the Apostles.

Preface of the Saints and Martyrs.

Preface of the Dead.

(free thanksgiving may always be added to the prefaces, before the conclusion, as indicated in the common preface, page 57)

PREFACES

of *Advent*

It is truly meet and right,
our joy and our salvation,
that we should at all times and in all places
give thanks unto Thee, O Lord, Holy Father,
Almighty, Everlasting God, through Christ our Lord.

For He is the Saviour, whom in Thy mercy and faithfulness
Thou didst promise to man after his fall, that
His truth might come to instruct the ignorant,
His holiness to purify sinners, His strength to sustain the weak.

Since the time is at hand
when He whom Thou sendest should come,
since the day of our deliverance
has begun to dawn,
full of confidence in Thy promises,
we exult with holy joy.

Wherefore,
with angels and archangels,
with thrones and dominions,
and with all the army of the hosts of Heaven,
we sing the hymn of Thy glory,
and, without ceasing, cry:
Holy . . .

of *Christmas*

It is truly meet and right,
our joy and our salvation,
that we should at all times and in all places
give thanks unto Thee, O Lord, Holy Father,
Almighty, Everlasting God.

Because by the mystery of the Incarnation,
the light of Thy glory
hath shone

69

with new splendour in our hearts;
and while we contemplate God
in a visible form,
we are taken up by Him
to the love of things invisible.

Wherefore,
with angels and archangels,
with thrones and dominions,
and with all the army of the hosts of Heaven,
we sing the hymn of Thy glory,
and, without ceasing, cry:
Holy . . .

of the Epiphany

It is truly meet and right,
our joy and our salvation,
that we should at all times and in all places
give thanks unto Thee, O Lord, Holy Father,
Almighty, Everlasting God.

Because when Thine only-begotten Son
manifestly appeared
in our mortal humanity,
He restored it by bringing to us
the new light of His immortal nature.

Wherefore,
with angels and archangels,
with thrones and dominions,
and with all the army of the hosts of Heaven,
we sing the hymn of Thy glory,
and, without ceasing, cry:
Holy . . .

It is truly meet and right,
our joy and our salvation,
that we should at all times and in all places
give thanks unto Thee, O Lord, Holy Father,
Almighty, Everlasting God.

Thou hast with a loud voice revealed Thyself to us
at the waters of Jordan,
to designate the Saviour from Heaven,
and to show Thyself
the Father of Everlasting Light.

Thou didst open the heavens,
pour out Thy blessing, purify the waters,
and, by the Holy Spirit
like a dove,
Thou didst proclaim Jesus: Thy Beloved Son.

The waters of baptism to-day
can bring Thy blessing
and take away our curse,
purify believers of all sin
and make them
sons of God the Father by adoption
unto eternal life;

By our birth in the flesh
we were destined for a temporal life,
by violation death took hold of us;
to-day we find eternal life again
and we are promised
the glory of the Kingdom of Heaven,
through Christ our Lord.

Wherefore,
with angels and archangels,
with thrones and dominions,
and with all the army of the hosts of Heaven,

we sing the hymn of Thy glory,
and, without ceasing, cry:
Holy . . .

of Sundays in Lent

It is truly meet and right,
our joy and our salvation,
that we should at all times and in all places
give thanks unto Thee, O Lord, Holy Father,
Almighty, Everlasting God, through Christ our Lord.

In whom Thou dost nourish our faith,
stimulate our hope
and fortify our love.

He is the true and living bread,
the food which gives eternity,
the nourishment which gives strength.

He is Thy Word, creator of all things;
by this bread was Moses Thy servant nourished
forty days,
when he received Thy law,
for Thy glory shone upon him,
Thy word and Thy spirit fed him.

Lord, evermore give us this bread,
and grant that we may ever hunger
after Christ, our Lord.

By whom the angels praise Thy majesty,
dominions worship Thee
and powers stand in awe;
the heavens and the heavenly hosts
and the blessed seraphim
united in one joy extol Thee;
with whose songs,
we pray Thee, join our voices
in one proclamation of Thy praise:
Holy . . .

It is truly meet and right,
our joy and our salvation,
that we should at all times and in all places
give thanks unto Thee, O Lord, Holy Father,
Almighty, Everlasting God.

Who didst with Thy presence nourish forty days,
Moses, Elijah and Thine only-begotten Son,
The Lord of the Law and the Prophets
and our Lord.

We implore Thy mercy,
that we may be filled with the joys
which Thy Son received
in this time of retreat;
and as we follow Him in His temptations,
so may His promises be fulfilled in us.

By Him the angels praise Thy majesty,
dominions worship Thee
and powers stand in awe;
the heavens and the heavenly hosts
and the blessed seraphim
united in one joy extol Thee;
with whose songs,
we pray Thee, join our voices
in one proclamation of Thy praise:
Holy . . .

of the Passion

It is truly meet and right,
our joy and our salvation,
that we should at all times and in all places
give thanks unto Thee, O Lord, Holy Father,
Almighty, Everlasting God.

For Thou didst affix to the wood of the Cross
the salvation of mankind,
through Christ our Lord,
who His own Self bare our sins
in His own body on the tree,
that we, being dead to our sins,
should live unto righteousness.

By Him the angels praise Thy majesty,
dominions worship Thee,
and powers stand in awe;
the heavens and the heavenly hosts
and the blessed seraphim,
united in one joy, extol Thee;
with whose songs,
we pray Thee, join our voices
in one proclamation of Thy praise:
Holy . . .

of Palm Sunday

It is truly meet and right,
our joy and our salvation,
that we should at all times and in all places
give thanks unto Thee, O Lord, Holy Father,
Almighty, Everlasting God, through Christ our Lord.

It was Thy good will that He should take human nature,
and fulfil all the prophesies
proclaimed by Holy Scripture,
from His birth at Bethlehem
until His entry into Jerusalem.

May our song ring out for Christ,
as the praises of the crowd
which came to meet Him,
for we are filled with love of Him.

We run the way of the Lord who cometh,
and, in company with the angels
and with all the Church,
we proclaim the hymn to Thy glory, saying:
Holy . . .

of Maundy Thursday

It is truly meet and right,
our joy and our salvation,
that we should at all times and in all places
give thanks unto Thee, O Lord, Holy Father,
Almighty, Everlasting God, through Christ our Lord,
the true High Priest for ever,
the only priest who knew no sin.

When at the Last Supper
He did institute the unending sacrifice of thanksgiving,
He offered first Himself to Thee,
and taught us first to offer
and receive.

Whenever we eat His flesh,
which was sacrificed for us, it strengtheneth us,
whenever we drink His blood,
which was shed for us, it purifieth us.

Wherefore,
with angels and archangels,
with thrones and dominions,
and with all the army of the hosts of Heaven,
we sing the hymn of Thy glory,
and, without ceasing, cry:
Holy . . .

F

of Easter

It is truly meet and right,
our joy and our salvation,
to praise Thee,
O Lord,
at all times,
but still more gloriously,
on this day (at this time),
when Christ our Passover was sacrificed.

For He is the true Paschal Lamb,
which hath taken away the sin of the world;
who by His death
hath destroyed death for us,
and by His rising again
hath restored to us life.

Wherefore,
with angels and archangels,
with thrones and dominions,
and with all the army of the hosts of Heaven,
we sing the hymn of Thy glory,
and, without ceasing, cry:
Holy . . .

of the Ascension

It is truly meet and right,
our joy and our salvation,
that we should at all times and in all places
give thanks unto Thee, O Lord, Holy Father,
Almighty, Everlasting God, through Christ our Lord.

Who, after His resurrection
visibly appeared to His disciples
and in their sight was taken up to Heaven,
that He might make us partakers of His divine nature.

76

Wherefore,
with angels and archangels,
with thrones and dominions,
and with all the army of the hosts of Heaven,
we sing the hymn of Thy glory,
and, without ceasing, cry:
Holy . . .

of Pentecost

It is truly meet and right,
our joy and our salvation,
that we should at all times and in all places
give thanks unto Thee, O Lord, Holy Father,
Almighty, Everlasting God, through Christ our Lord.

Who, ascending above all heavens,
and sitting at Thy right hand,
shed forth (as upon this day)
the promised Holy Spirit
upon the children of adoption.

Wherefore,
in all the world
all creatures with exceeding joy
exult.
While the heavenly hosts
and the angelic powers
together sing,
and endlessly repeat the hymn of Thy glory:
Holy . . .

of the Trinity

It is truly meet and right,
our joy and our salvation,
that we should at all times and in all places
give thanks unto Thee, O Lord, Holy Father,
Almighty, Everlasting God.

Who, with Thine only-begotten Son and the Holy Spirit
art one God,
one Lord.

For that which by Thy revelation
we believe of Thy Glory,
the same we affirm
of Thy Son, and of the Holy Spirit,
without any difference.

By angels and archangels
Thou art sung,
by cherubim and seraphim,
who cease not
daily with one voice to cry:
Holy . . .

of the Church

It is truly meet and right,
our joy and our salvation,
that we should at all times and in all places
give thanks unto Thee, O Lord, Holy Father,
Almighty, Everlasting God.

For Thou,
the Giver of all good things,
inhabitest this house of prayer,
and never ceasest
with Thy grace to sanctify
the Church which Thou Thyself didst found.

The Church is the true house of prayer,
the temple of Thy glory,
the seat of never-failing truth,
the sanctuary of eternal love.
She is the ark, which saveth us from the flood
to bring us to the haven of salvation.

She is the only well-beloved bride
whom Christ bought for Himself
with His own blood,
and vivifieth with His spirit.

She is our mother,
who by Thy grace hath borne us unto new life,
by her we are nourished with Thy Word,
strengthened with the bread of life.
gladdened by the help of Thy mercy.

Finally, she is, through Christ,
faithful and militant on earth,
and, crowned by Him,
eternally triumphant in the heavens.

Wherefore,
with angels and archangels,
with thrones and dominions,
and with all the army of the hosts of Heaven,
we sing the hymn of Thy glory,
and, without ceasing, cry:
Holy . . .

It is truly meet and right,
our joy and our salvation,
to hymn Thee, bless Thee, praise Thee,
give thanks unto Thee and worship Thee.
For Thou only art God,
Thou and Thine only-begotten Son, with the Holy Ghost.

Thou hast brought us
into being out of nothing,
Thou hast raised us
when we were fallen;
Thou ordereth all things, without ceasing,
that Heaven may be open for us,
and Thy Kingdom, which cometh, granted to us.

For all Thy benefits
we give thanks unto Thee,
and to Thine only-begotten Son
with the Holy Spirit.

O Thou whom angels and archangels serve,
cherubim and seraphim,
who sing
the hymn of Thy victory and proclaim it, saying:
Holy . . .

of Unity

It is truly meet and right,
our joy and our salvation,
that we should at all times and in all places
give thanks unto Thee, O Lord, Holy Father,
Almighty, Everlasting God, through Christ our Lord.

Who on the eve of His passion,
prayed for the unity of all faithful people,
in Him and in Thee,
by the Holy Spirit in the Church;
we believe that Thou wilt hear His prayer.

We give thanks unto Thee
for the unity of the body of Christ,
and we await with joy
the day when we shall perfectly be one,
that the world may know that Thou hast sent
Thy Son
and that He loved us as Thou didst love Him.

Wherefore,
with angels and archangels,
with thrones and dominions,
and with all the army of the hosts of Heaven,
we sing the hymn of Thy glory,
and, without ceasing, cry:
Holy . . .

of Christ the King

It is truly meet and right,
our joy and our salvation,
that we should at all times and in all places
give thanks unto Thee, O Lord, Holy Father,
Almighty, Everlasting God.

Who with the unction of the Holy Spirit
didst anoint Thine only-begotten Son,
Jesus Christ, our Lord,
to be a Priest for ever, and King of all the world,
that, offering Himself
an unspotted sacrifice of peace
upon the altar of the Cross,
He might accomplish the mystery of man's salvation.

And, subjecting to His power
all creatures,
might deliver up to Thine Infinite Majesty
an eternal and universal kingdom,
a kingdom of truth and life,
a kingdom of sanctity and grace,
a kingdom of justice, peace and love.

Wherefore,
with angels and archangels,
with thrones and dominions,
and with all the army of the hosts of Heaven,
we sing the hymn of Thy glory,
and, without ceasing, cry:
Holy . . .

of the Virgin Mary

It is truly meet and right,
our joy and our salvation,
that we should at all times and in all places
give thanks unto Thee, O Lord, Holy Father,
Almighty, Everlasting God,
and that we should praise Thee, bless Thee,
and celebrate Thee
upon the . . . (Annunciation, Visitation, Festival)
of the Blessed Virgin Mary.

Because that by the overshadowing of the Holy Ghost
she conceived Thine only-begotton Son,
and brought into the world the light eternal,
Jesus Christ, our Lord.

By whom the angels praise Thy Majesty,
dominions adore Thee,
and powers stand in awe;
the heavens and the heavenly hosts,
and the blessed seraphim,
united in one joy extol Thee.
With whose songs,
we pray Thee, join our voices
in one proclamation of Thy praise:
Holy . . .

of the Apostles

It is truly meet and right,
our joy and our salvation,
that we, O Lord, should humbly entreat Thee,
the Everlasting Shepherd,
not to forsake Thy flock;
keep it under Thy continual protection
by the word of Thy holy apostles:
that Thy flock may ever be guided
by these same leaders,
whom Thou didst choose to continue Thy work,
and place as shepherds at its head.

Wherefore,
with angels and archangels,
with thrones and dominions,
and with all the army of the hosts of Heaven,
we sing the hymn of Thy glory,
and, without ceasing, cry:
Holy . . .

It is truly meet and right,
our joy and our salvation,
that we should at all times and in all places
give thanks unto Thee, O Lord, Holy Father,
Almighty, Everlasting God.
Who in the assembly of the saints
dost find Thy glory,
and, crowning their works,
dost crown Thine own good gifts.

Thou dost wish their lives
to serve us as examples,
that in communion with them
we may be made to share their riches
and be assisted by their prayers;
that we, being encompassed about
with so great a cloud of witnesses,
might run without fainting
to the battle that is set before us,
and receive with them
the crown of glory that fadeth not away,
through Jesus Christ, our Lord,
by whose blood
we have access to the Eternal Kingdom.

By whom the angels,
trembling, praise Thy majesty,
and all the choirs of heavenly spirits,
united in one joy, extol Thee.
With whose songs,
we pray Thee, join our voices
in one proclamation of Thy praise:
Holy . . .

It is truly meet and right,
our joy and our salvation,
that we should at all times and in all places
give thanks unto Thee, O Lord, Holy Father,
Almighty, Everlasting God,
through Christ our Lord.

In whom hath shone forth for us
the hope of a blessed resurrection.
That if the thought of certain death
dismay us,
we might be encouraged
by the promise of immortal life to come.

For to Thy faithful people, Lord,
life is transformed and not destroyed;
and, at the disappearance
of the tabernacle of our earthly sojourning,
a dwelling-place eternal
awaiteth us in Heaven.

Wherefore,
with angels and archangels,
with thrones and dominions,
and with all the army of the hosts of Heaven,
we sing the hymn of Thy glory,
and, without ceasing, cry:
Holy . . .